AF207882

There Three

Devin King

Kenning Editions

2020

THREE

THERE

there

twel

Copyright © 2020 by Devin King

CLOPS was previously published by The Green Lantern Press. *The Resonant Space* and *These Necrotic Ethos Come the Plains* were originally published by Holon Press.

Published by Kenning Editions
3147 W Logan Blvd., Suite 7, Chicago, IL 60647

Kenningeditions.com

Distributed by Small Press Distribution
1341 Seventh St., Berkeley, CA 94710
Spdbooks.org

ISBN 978-0-9997198-9-3
Library of Congress Control Number: 2019953119

Designed by Crisis

Kenning Editions is a 501c3 non-profit, independent literary publisher
investigating the relationships of aesthetic quality to political commitment.
Consider donating or subscribing: Kenningeditions.com/shop/donation

To begin.

I built something in which I hid. Others were there, inside this thing I built, safe with their trust inside this thing I built. Their trust and this thing I built, all that kept us safe. Others ignored this thing I built and slept and this thing I built and the trust of those with me kept us alive as we slaughtered those who ignored this thing I built. During the slaughter, this thing I built was an empty thing, this thing I built, though others' trust for the thing I built filled this thing I built, making this thing I built a thing I built.

To begin, there was the war.

In these letters are letters and I was one among. So was he, that man of rage. I kissed him and from him I took a shield. The world was hammered into it with the ocean as a ring. Later I used the shield as my raft.
And upon my friend's shield I lived among islands as my thought's eye

seeing my love naked in a city burning seeing my love with one eye poked out seeing my love killing the sun's oxen seeing my love letting go of the wind seeing my love flying through rocks seeing my love naked in a cave seeing my love naked in a cave seeing my love naked in a cave to see my love draped around a tree

In Penelope's letters were letters and I was one among memories she wrote and quoted for me,

Both here and

there,

part of
something   I am not.

4

To begin, there was the war.

I was woken angrily in the night. I prayed to the goddess of the city. I mustered my friend. He prayed to the goddess of the city. We saw him coming. We lay with the corpses. He did not see us among them as he passed. We chased after him. He thought us another. He turned to our smiles. They were not for him. We wounded him so he would bow to us. He bowed to us.

—What do you attempt? He said he spied to gain my friend's horses.

—Where do the others sleep? He told us where his friend with horses slept. My friend killed him. We went and found the man and his horses. My friend killed him. I mounted his horses. I rode them as my own. I thanked the goddess of the city for such fine horses. I thanked the goddess of the city for such fine horses.

To begin, there was the war.

When my friend came back he had his lover's blood on his hands, his tunic—he had blood everywhere, and his body was the most beautiful thing I had ever seen, an olive turning into wine. I took him in my arms and I dipped him in the ocean and he looked up at me and he called me his mother. It wasn't anything but a kind of windlessness. I was glad for it, then.

—If we turn around we'll see a thousand boys learning how to swim from the shore. But we didn't and I guess that's when the argument started.

—They should turn around and learn how to kill.

—Not without rest. Later I won my dead friend's armour against a man who fell.

To begin, there was the war.

Another one took me out of myself. That one, coming after another one, said I was not in the horse I built, that I led the horse forward to the city's walls, that I waited. And that is enough to give me pause. But I led them to the city and I was with them in the horse. I was with them in the horse and I led them to the city. I knocked on the gate and I felt my friends' sweat become my own. And we waited and, late, the city opened and took us inside.

1

To begin, there was the war.

This city is a city and it is built for us and we have come for the city. In the city there are streets and they are paved for us and we run along them. In the city there are doors and they are built for us and we break them down. In the city there are rooms and they are built for us and we wreck them. In the city there are men and they are built for us and we kill them and count them. In the city there are women and they are built for us and we rape them and count them. In the city there are children and they are built for us and we show them our swords and show them our shoulders and show them our arms and hands and show them our legs and feet and show them our hips and show them our cocks and show them our horses and count them. And show them our horses and count them.

In the city, my friend and I run up the ramp and we see a building next to us. I want to use my hands and before me lies a child and I pick the child up with my hands and this child, I lift this child with my hands and I place him in the building and the building sways gently and I kiss the building and the building kisses me. My friend calls my name and the building says go with him go with him go with him. We find the stairs and we see a building next to us. We run up the stairs. My friend says something. And we sit quickly and eat the dried apricots. My friend finishes and he stands up and he takes my sore arms and he pulls me up and we jump from ledge to ledge. Each ledge is attached to a window and we look through them. Here is what I hear through the windows.

—Sea, brine, breaker, seducer, star of the sea.

—This is a list of things I found in my body.

—Full of people, there is nothing more to do than this, to be full of people.

—And we come to be when those who left return.

—20 of them, all dead today in a roadside.

—This is the this is the this is the.

There is another window and I will return to it. To be safe. I am not sure if my friend heard the same things I did, but I am certain we saw the same things. Someone speaking naked and in a frenzy. Right now my friend and I are jumping from ledge to ledge and in the room in front of me is a light on and in the bed there is a naked body and the the girl girl is is sleeping sleeping.

From the ledges my friend and I jumped and we are, suddenly, on the other side of the building. We see the goddess of the city in the building's side and we thank her and we listen and she sings to us, alone and above:

Ooooohhhhhhhhh Yoooouuuu Chiiiihhhhhhld,
Will you lead me to the king's palace,
The place where the stories are told?
Fear not the darkened alleys,
But if I may be so bold . . .
Oooooohhhhhhhhh Yoooouuuu Chiiiihhhhhhld,
Will you lead me to the king's palace,
The place where the stories are told?

11

We hear breathing and we look down at them and there they lay. All of them, in rows. The soldiers' gasp a thousand, the soldiers' gasp a thousand, the soldiers' gasp a thousand, the soldiers' gasp a thousand's song:

Oooooohhhhhhhhh Yoooouuuu Chiiiihhhhhhld,
We'll lead you to the king's palace,
Through streets paved by men,
Fear not that swords may greet you,
Be bold, they'll let you in.
Oooooohhhhhhhhh Yoooouuuu Chiiiihhhhhhld,
We'll lead you to the king's palace,
through streets paved by men.

My friend and I face a choice and we each choose a song and we each choose our own song and I will see him later I know. But I will never hold him again and now I hold him to me but his strong arms lift me up and I feel my lips on his brow and I kiss him I kiss him and he moves my body in the air and I dance alone dangling all elbows in his arms and he stands a giant and I float a man and I sing my friend my newly learned lullaby:

rug room

wife's toes

stretch cherry child

uniform.

from home

eat ours,

upstairs

fed well

shiver hips twist in the bed.

I feel my friend relax and I fall into his chest and he sings me his dreams:

silence my deep silent pink wishes.
heave heave little messes
heave heave little chores
silence my deep silent pink wishes.

silence sinks,   silence dishes.

silence papers   and
silence looks.

silence kisses,   silence nieces,

silence mores.   silence pictures,   silence notes,
silence pens, silence letters to write to silent friends,
silence daughters,
silence wives,
silence sons,
silence lives,
silence shoes,
silence floors, silence tables,

14

silence doors,

silence beds, silence snores.

And he rests to wake and fight. And I run to return to the room. To be safe.

15

Balancing on the ledge, into the lit room sight broke by no bedclothes the naked body becoming. Breaking the window, into the lit room broke the body's sight by the bed the naked body broke by no one but my body breaking the body

I grow excited by the movement, the change, I grow excited by the movement. I go to her and I pull her out of bed I fuck my wife in a bed and I will fuck this woman against the desk, this is a rich man's house, this large desk, and I push her against her husband's desk, a senator's desk, and I grab his weight and I hold her throat with his weight and the papers fly around us and stick to us and I push myself inside this woman and I feel a ring and I pick it up and I push myself inside this woman and I put his signet on my finger and I push myself inside this woman and I push down on her throat with this weight and I push myself inside this woman and I stamp her with this signet on my finger on her breasts and I push myself inside this woman and I stamp her with this signet on my finger on her thighs and on her belly and I push down on her throat with this weight and I push myself inside this woman and stamp her with this signet on my finger on her

I tie a cloth around my eyes I plug my ears
with fibered wax I bruise my hands with
pine cones and I think of Penelope on this
desk in front of me and a still light
a still red light comes.

a red note
    bred
among

      agencies.

To begin, there was the troth. I was woken angrily in the night. There is a man in our room and you look for me and you see me inside of a horse and you see me in a city burning and you see me. But he takes my arms and he holds me down. And he kisses you, this man kisses my arms and I look for you and I see you inside of a horse and I see you in a city burning and I see you. But he takes my legs and he holds me down. And he kisses you, this man kisses my legs and I look for you and I see you inside of a horse and I see you in a city burning and I see you. But he takes my breasts and he holds me down. And he kisses you, this man kisses my breasts and I look for you and I see you inside of a horse and I see you in a city burning and I see you. But he takes my body out of you and I fall and they hold you down and I become a ranking line and I lose your words and I turn away from you this man turns me away from you and we sit unable to speak to each other and my love, I have left this thing we built and have gone into a city burning.

May I come to your bed now?

You may not.

But I strung *my* bow.

You have.

And I have killed these suitors.

You have.

What else will you ask of me?

I want you to move my bed.

20

Later, ears cottoned with constant sound, I walk through the city, under the bridge, and out into the water where the sea otters squirm and float. Their bellies are naked and white. They laugh and speak in a water dialect, waves are nouns, foam participles, and sand the conjunction. The otters keep me calm singing their stories but I have arms and cannot not swim like their heroes. Together we all joke and giggle, point and make faces, eat pretzels and chocolate. How else are we to make of ourselves something so foreign? By lying?

I almost forget the city but the otters remind me of it in the last of their songs. Amongst the city-songs I hear my name and I see my body and in me the otters' water wells. I take up the song and sing a new verse about how I will find my way home to my wife.

One of my arms begins to paddle and I swim in circles. The salt from my spit mixes with the sea. The otters' daughter births a son into my arms. They name me godfather to him and, as children do, he begins acting out my stories.

He grows to be a great politician and on a fall evening parents, grandparents, and I eat supper around the politician's silver table inlaid with broken pottery. His grandparents nod off and the politician asks each of us to sing him stories. We smoke cigars and the politician's father sings to him of his birth. We eat gelato and the politician's mother sings to him of his dead relatives. We drink wine and I sing to him of how I will find my way home to my wife. He laughs and takes me into his den to show me the costumes, hanging and musty, that he had once acted out my songs in. I blink and ask him what he did with them now. He said,

—I will show you. And he put on a robe. And he grabbed a shield. And he grabbed a sword. And he grabbed a horse. And he begins to act out tales. My tales.

In a child's pantomime I see myself and I
hide under my cowl so I do not have to see
and I cry.

To begin, there was the troth.

In these letters are letters and I was one among. So was my love, that man of cunning. I kissed him and from him I took a horse. The world was hammered into it and when I rode it I used the ocean as my spurs. Later I knelt at the horse and used it as my loom.

And upon my love's horse I lived with him as my thought's eye

seeing my love naked in a city burning
seeing my love with one eye poked out
seeing my love killing the sun's oxen
seeing my love letting go of the wind
seeing my love flying through rocks
seeing my love naked in a cave seeing my love naked in a cave seeing my love naked in a cave to see my love draped around a tree

In Odysseus' letters were letters and I was one among memories he wrote and quoted for me;

Both here and
there,

part of
something   I am not.

To begin, there was the troth.

I woke up and have not been able to leave my house for years. The girls dress me and feed me and I throw love at my son and he walks towards the hall with the men. Around my feet. I sit down and pull myself up to the work of remembering you. And in the memories of your flesh your flesh is able to become my flesh again and my flesh became your memory, coming with it. And we went to my loom and I wove your tales for you. You were coming home to me. And I was stuck, at my loom. And I grew angry and I grew angry and I unwove your stories and I tossed the thread in the fire. And I put my flesh to the fire. I will burn you from me. But you will not burn, you became a wax and you gummed my skin. And I slept with you upon my skin. And in the morning I could not breath and I gathered up your residue and began again.

25

To begin, there was the troth.
It's dark and I am fingering the weave of
you and it rips and I know I've found a way
to keep the men from me. And to do that
is to have to start over with you in the
morning.

To begin, there was the troth.
You come upon my island and I am there
and I pick you up and I pick your friends
up and I take you to my cave and I leave
my cave and I put a rock in my cave's door
and you cannot leave. In the fields I move
among the sheep and with soft fur they
tickle my feet. And I fall into the earth and
I feel them graze upon my body, rubbing
at my pores. One steps onto my face and
I grab him with my hand and I stand up out
of the earth. I will cook us a feast. And I
walk back to

the cave and I come upon the

rock and I put the sheep down

and I move the rock and I

pick the sheep up and

I feel the jabbing in my eye.

27

To begin, there was the troth.

You come to my island and I let you walk

upon it. I let you walk upon my island. You

find my sheep and you take my sheep and

you kill my sheep. I grow and I grow angry

and I pick you up. And I pick your friend

up. You have many friends and I pick them

all up. I hold you in my hand and the rest

are in my pocket. I carry you to my cave

and I put them in my cave screaming and

I hold you for a moment longer I hold you

for a moment longer in my fist and you

stare at me asking and I think

What if this man, this

thoughtful man, what if this

man, this thoughtful man,

thought this thoughtful man,

this thoughtful man, man this

thoughtful man thinks his

way out of my cave? And I

place you down with the

rest of them and I place a

boulder at the door and I

walk through my island

and I lie with my sheep.

To begin, there was the troth.
And I ask you your name and you say, "No-
body." And I see your smile and I say, "No
sir, really, what is your name?" and you
say, "No, ma'am no, no really my name is
Nobody." And I laugh and I feel your small
hand upon my back and I blush and your
smile I feel your smile in my ear and you
say, "Nobody," and you were small and I
let you walk upon my body and I ask you
where you had gotten that name and on
my collarbone you smile and say, "Where
every son is named, in his mother's arms,"
and I let you walk upon me and I ask you
where you had been born and on my ribs
you smile smiled your smile you smiled
and said, "Where every son is born, in his
mother's stomach," and I let you walk
upon me and I asked you why you had
come
                    to visit me and inside of me
you smile your smile smile your you you
        smile smile

                                your smile you smile your
            smile you smiled and said,

"Why every man comes to visit you,"

            and I felt a

            burning in my eye and I was

                  blind and I called for you and

                        I said, "Nobody," and

I felt

                      for you and I only felt

moving cloth

        and I called for you and I said, "Nobody," and I only felt

moving cloth   and I called for you and I   said, "Nobody," and I

threw   rocks into the sea and you

           were gone.

The Resorts Space

Herman's Hermits, being

  rubbed by women   in front of

giant cutouts of   black and white ladyheads.   I really expected the dude

  in the glasses

to be like   "fuck off,

     I'm trying to

play a fucking song"

    {which,

might be,

      expressed   in the term

"absence of

prodigality" the window

  beside Lindner's

desk . . . adorned} *against*

  what light

is false   *what breath*

sucked . . . ah! they return those secret gold killers who

seen those

  English

dramas

  too-

who

Matt sent me twenty five cassette tapes
in the mail today, and I'm having
a hard time opening the door
cause I put lotion on
for the first time ever.

                            :—Festspielhaus—:,

                            :—Festspielhaus—:,

what sort of noir
does Peter Konwitschny direct?
I saw his *Cosi*
fan Tutti on YouTube
and there were mooses
eating sherbet with spoons.
The opera's title, translated:
Thus do all women.

                            :—Festspielhaus—:,

                            :—Festspielhaus—:,

when my roommate with sunglasses
got home he opened it
and asked me, "why didn't
you ask the neighborhood kids?"
And when we got upstairs
Rebecca opened the door wide
and asked me, "why didn't
you just ring the buzzer?"
The three of us stood
there and began making dinner.

Requiem for Lux Interior/
Ducktail for Louis Zukofsky

you don't *sho'nuff*
yes I do the
men yell on

the radio *a*
thick radio broadcast
signal slurs myth Lux
Interior dead, just

like you, *hollers*
"radioactive"
you said it!

a *haht rodda's* dream, parking with C & P
19 months old, your kid plays violin
ferchrissakes
who said it!

much faster than *I* could ever say it
the engineer's slapback
on your voice elides
and pops

cracking gum
rolling your filterless
up in your shirtsleeve

go billy go billy

go billy go billy

go billy go billy

go ba rock a billy

you ain't never caught a rabbit

vs.

you, *ain't never*, caught a rabbit

Upped young men

comb grease their hair

rewrite A/10:

"Poor songster so weak

Stopped singing to curse

A mess sucked out

No substance

[   ] tunes in the [   ] broadcast

People   people   people

But you record it

There is no whisper but vibrates

Your body

People   people   people

The [   ] radio calls to you in [   ]

to help [   ]"   People   people   people

Rock me
   bae-bay
Alana wants
   all night
to talk
   about
laminae
   I don't
know what
   to do
Next time
   bae-bay
but chooses
darling,
   darling,
mica,
darling,
   hatred,
darling
   exoteric,
   and pure
gest rhythm darling
      Skeet-
   er Davis 1958 broken
arms and legs—car crash.

Her sister Betty Jack dead.
Her sister Georgia takes her place
along-
side Skeeter
in the first harmonic girl group to
hit Nº 1 with

<brth | hrmns>
　　　　　I Forgot More Than You'll Ever Know About Him:

You think
　You know
the smile on
　his lip
the thrill at the touch
　of his fingertips
but I forgot more
　than you'll ever know
about him

Jeff's
　fainting
Believe me buddy
　I ain't no fool
naked in a western
　neighborhood,
I made the money
　working after school
we get in a car
　and find him

in twenty bent
    over a trashcan
puking,
    Jeff's fainting
in a western neighborhood

Jeff's fainting naked in a commuter neighborhood—
his frantic texts illumine the table's plates.
Alana tells Micah, who's reading the journal
about the Russian artists who create sports,
and you borrow the keys between sips.
Our hands decoct Skeeter's 1958 car crash
gest on the radio; we see Jeff
bald, exoteric, puking against those passive houses
AJ stole from Europe to build here
(he showed us how little heat escapes—
superinsulation, lack of thermal bridges, airtightness, space-
heating, earth warming tubes, with no radiators,
there's more space on the rooms' walls—
and saw Blixa picking apples in the market.

        lord crank and hoist and hoist and crank

              lord crank and hoist and hoist and crank).

Micah's reading aloud as the door opens,
"The metropolitan reader's flattery of the exotic,"
and when he hands a cup to Jeff
Jeff opens his fist and drinks.

Rock me
 bae-bay
I'd like
 all night
to talk
 about
Blue Cheer
I don't
know what
 to do
Next time
 bae-bay
but choose
darling,
 darling,
music
with un-
 druggéd
words, so-
 ber words
darling,
 carrying
hatred,
darling,
 with them,
exoteric,

and pure,
Betty
   Jack Dav-
is dies
   August
car crash
   1953
number
   one The
Davis
   Sisters
number
the first
   harmonic
girl group
   to reach
   number
   one
I can't
   believe
the love
   for me
is
   buried
number
   one The
Davis
   Sisters
number
   two,
Skeeter

        Davis
saved from
    breathing,
broken
    arms, legs
her sist-
    er dead
Betty
Jack
Davis
number
one
1953

I Forgot More Than You'll Ever Know
    About him
You think
You know the smile on his lips the thrill at the touch of his fingertips but I forgot more than
you'll ever know about him you think you'll find a heaven of bliss in each caress each tender
kiss but I forgot more than you'll ever know about him you stole his love from me one day
you didn't care how you hurt me but you can never steal away memories of what used to
be you think he's yours to have and to hold some day you'll learn when his life grows cold
that I forgot more than you'll ever know about him you think he's yours to have and to hold
some day you'll learn when his life grows cold that I forgot more than you'll ever know
about him

Skeeter
    Davis
saved from
    breathing
broken

arms, legs
sings with
number
one The
Davis
Sisters
number
three,
Betty Jack's
sister,
Georgia,
sings
in her
dead
sister's
place
1953
number
one The
Davis
Sisters
number
the first
harmonic
girl group
to reach
number
one

Sean buys cook-
    ies in the
sun when they're
    melting al-
ready, ac-
    quiring blem-
ishes, like
    videos,
born from move-
    ment, scanning
themselves, the
    virtue of
being cop-
    ied themselves,
    conquering
the appa-
    ratus in
likeness. Lab-
    ility
lightness rap-
    idity.
Pronouncing
    is an ac-
tivity;
"that most im-
    portant ques-

tion from the
  seventies:
which is more
  important
sound or im-
  age?"
  visual flut-
tering at-
  taining speed,
doing my
  "I feel awk-
ward about
  ordering
foods with sil-
  ly names" bit
while the kid
  in the tree
at the park
  sings hippie
songs loudly
  un-peacea-
bly singing
  hippie songs
in the park
  loudly *I*
don't need from
  you a wat-
erfall of
  careless praise . . .
but all I
  want is your

eyes in the
   morning as
we wait for
   a short while.
Outside the
   audito-
rium Tim

of pock-

et cor-

  net trace-

s our

  color,

brown col-

  or, brown

color

  brown

lebens-

  spur brown—

Dr. Poo

  Pah Doo

of Des-

  tine Tam-

bourine

  brown

the lim-

  inal

Dr. John,

  brown,

  "transcribes

his pri-

  vate pon-

dering

  into

public
   print . . . He
sort[s]
   through his
memo-
   ries and
the nat-
   ural
scene be-
   fore him."
   §
exhib
   it a
pattern
   of myst-
ic as-
   cent, mat-
ter a-
   gainst ground
ground mat-
   ter the
love cults,
   "Distant,"
we say,
   "Distant
and thwart-
   ed post-
scripts of
   time tra-
vel—the
   love cults,"

we sneer,
   "the love
cults," we
   sneer, dis-
tant, now,
   the sec-
onds twist,
   our e-
rasers,
   the bi-
derec-
   tional
erasers
   tossing
pencils
   at lur-
king cork.
   §
The score,
   (the piano)
or pro-
   to con-
cepts? The
   shrilling
booth of
   the in-
sect sell-
   er, a
vivid
   confi-
dence, no,

-arktoi-

claw out

my eyes

-arktoi-

not tou-

ring -ark-

toi- but

serial-

ly res-

ident,

the un-

relie-

ved grue-

some sent-

iment-

alit-

y of

the stuff

we were

playing.

There is

the use

of the

piano,

no long-

er mel-

odic,

or can-

tabile,

but so-

lid, u-

nified
as one
　drum. I
mean *sin-*
　gle sounds
produ-
　ced by
multi-
　ple im-
pact; as
　distinct
from chords,
　which are
in sort
　of chains
or slush-
　es of
sound,
　of pock-
et cor-
　net trace-
s, this
　sound, this
tepid
　dance, this
slow ver-
　sion of
the true
　Prote-
us of
　nature.

§
Gabor's
  machine
alters
  the dur-
ation
  of a
sound with-
out shift-
  ing its
pitch, when
  the god
of the
  vege-
tation
  myths dies.

that most im-
    portant ques-
tion from the
    seventies:
which is more
    important
sound or im-
    age?
Maybe a
    quiet night
in Chatta-
    nooga or
a Wild Sat-
    urday night
in Memphis
    we'll find our
selves before
    a piano,
find that our
    mouths are mov-
ing maybe

Forgive
  Ross his
acous-
  matic
posting
  histor-
y, he's
  still think-
ing a-
  bout MJ,
about
  "specific moments of illumination,
directions
  which are always
precise and always
  reveal
a new
  aspect
of the ob-
  ject,
    towards
which our
  attention
is deliberately or unconsciously drawn,"
  finally through the roof
on to somewhere ne-

ar

and far in time

    Rebecca snips her black hair and crumples

white paper in a gallery in Philadelphia

and "indeed could this sound fragment be

described

    in itself, when the "causal" and anecdotal perception was soon over and when it pre-

sented itself to the listener as an "object", always identical yet always capable of revealing

new characteristics when heard over and over again?"

"A Schnabel paradox is often commented upon:

that he professed to despise recordings, especially

for their musical fixity. "The variety seems"

pragmat-

  ic dear,

    sulpher

to the

  ears, red,

yellow

  and clev-

er, sus-

  taining

a be-

  leif in

rigid

  lost time,

where boys

  with mous-

taches

  play hands

of cards

  and in-

sult each

other
publ| |
ly oft-
en, only
  carrot,
only
  carrot
darling
  orange
this or-
  ange
carrot
  darling,
this lim-
  inal
taproot
and
  rosette and she got
  a cam-
era, and she got
photographs
  and she got
lithe pho-
  tographs
she got
lithe pho-
  tographs
of
the beautiful workers scrubbing the inside of human sized bubble they built and tested in
Isaac's back yard, "and here I am, making up different ways for dudes to sit politely and
in the woods."

Why, the decision on your part, to learn to sing

Takeshi Mizutani's guitar feedback is a circle built from tangents. Each tangent is the center of a two-dimensional vector-star that moves in vortices outwards and these stars can never touch except by violence. But the listener holds on to a secret, mongrel nature that expects the reverse in his musical substance; to them, Mizutani's feedback becomes the stock characters of a post-war play or short story and the blank centers of the costumed stars enact a strange form of passive discipline, the irreversible move- ments of destined emotion, and

Aaron,

who told me about how he cut his hair is
   driving
from Cal-
   ifor
nia to
   Chica-
go, film-
   ing bands
who use
 corroding tape for
a mag-
   azine.
My friend,
     Aaron
   who works
at im-

prints

for one thousand two hundred and sixty days and

  still talks about how

when his

  mother

remar-

  ried, he

became

  a ras-

ta with

  her,

or how,

often,

  I throw

myself

  off of

skyscrap-

  ers, or

cliffs, I

  make foods

up and

  sometimes

they don't

  taste like

anything—

  just like

hitting

  twelve notes

at a

  time. Son-

ia,

lost her

job, she

opened

a bou-

tique to

create

a rit-

ual, van-

quished by

death, her

re-

signed smile

seeking

Pseudo

terri-

tory,

paro-

dies, teach-

ing coll-

ege in

the Neth-

erlands:

The His-

tory

of Air-

ports *and*

when she

asks me

which one

I love

the best

I tear
open
  my shirt
and there's
  Rosie
on my
  chest.

"I have in mind objects whose outputs evoked by inputs in turn, function as *inputs* for subsequent states of the object," the final glorious chord of a romantic symphony captured and transformed into a continuous plateau, progressing from magnetic time that takes a pseudonym online and says that

he was paid to be angry over
the origin of Aztec cannibalism, was it
driven to because of a protein deficiency?
Rebecca thinks to herself: *Let me get*
this right. I gotta hang out, like,
deeply, with jihadi terrorists? and exploit that
relation to classify Sam as a gorilla?
Were they prime as goats which lead
directly to the door of truth?

one can acquire
                an addiction
                to goggles.
Take some
  human
action,
  say, a

theft, that
  tic in
England's
  hymning
of itself—
pure bard
  of the
pure, *Par-*
  sifal,
Sarah
      projects the lamp, stomps on dust
in her thick high heels, her face
is blank but she's seriously frowning guys
in her purple socks, her short pants.
She pours water into fifteen plastic cups
and hangs pieces of paper with text
that be-
lieves the
  past to
be a
  somewhat
better
  place:
"You
  can't help
a corpse
  . . . no one
can help
  any-
one."
  For example, if an unqualified generation was

being generated at some time, then also   <rsttl>
the thing in unqualified generation was being
gener-
ated.

       I am thrown into prison because I owned a watch. Or how,
  one day,
he came
  home—the
way he
  curved his
arm, the
  scar or
arrow—
  light
kindles
  light
like the
  hair of
corpses
  floating
in dus-
  ky wa-
ter, or
  that South
Hampton
  presents
itself
  as a
puzzle to us, "bad recording
equipment on the east coast,
and you want it in

a barn."
They built my city on top of a grave,
WABX
  and
WKNR
  in De-
troit serv-
  ed as
slender
  lifelines,
and on
  Fridays
she'd be
  there and
on Wed-
  nesday
not at
  all just
casu-
  ally
appear
  ing from
the clock
  across
the hall
how I left it,
  which has called me
how I left it,
  which has called me
how I left it—
we're gonna do a song that you've never   *<jy lctrnc>*

heard before
one day,
he came
home—
"To what
trials
must we
submit
ourselves
to make
ourselves
capa-
ble of
under-
standing
you and
getting
you to
speak?"
The scar
or ar-
row—light
kindles
light, her
brailed
up top-
sails, her
objects
which clut-
tered up
the shelf,

and found

the pack-

et of

cotton

wool,

now,

throughout,

they both

please and

displease.

Nobod-

y talks

peace, Luke,

"you get

a ver-

y bor-

ing sound

and sounds

wander

across"

his ska-

lly cap,

his Ex-

pos hat,

and, one

can im-

agine

a fourth

hat, the

saying

You're a

"

You're a

  You're a

   You're a

       pitch, magnetic and cumbersome and receding, an object interpretable in

relation to

    another through a third

You, Luke, You're a:

  Dino,

    Desi,

     and Billy,

        beautiful sons of the famous singers' letterpressed

        sense of entitlement, sense of filial worth, working

        in the sky a pair of shape of lights blinds brightest

        millions of jet black eyes . . . 1971 humans . . . atrophy

or

        Welcome to the camp, I guess you all know why

        we're here, my name is Tommy and I became aware

        this year, if you want to follow me, you've got to play

          pinball

You're a musician pressing a button on a keyboard to make your sample play over the PA

        Sue me Jack Sue me Sue me Jack

        Sue me Jack Sue me Sue me Jack

        Sue me Jack Sue me Sue me Jack

        Sue me Jack Sue me Sue me Jack

        I'm

        I'm on the left

        left side

        My

        My silhouette

        can't be touched

  you're

67

at peace,
you're tear-
    ing buil-
dings down
    peaceful-
ly, act-
    ually,
If I had my ways
You can
    leave the
village
    in the
morning,
    "I've got
        a job,"
whispers
    Peter,
        "I've got
            a job,
a drum-
    mer, ask-
    ed me
to watch
    his house
this week
    and may-
be the
    next and
I get
    to play
Basho

loudly

Venus

in Can-

 cer, Song

for the

 Queen; take care my love, the way to the castle is dark and long"

he's off film-

 ing in

a mod-

 ernist

house in,

 in Ken-

 tucky,

                     <thrswrldwhrcngndtllmscrtst>

 Mike Love

is wearing

 Mary beads and sing-

ing nasally,

               She was the first to ever love me, the

               first to hold me to her breast, god bless

               her because she is my mother, she'll be

               the last one I forget

a comb-

 ina-

tion of

 a tool

and the

 human

mind, a ref-

 erence

made in

slow churn-
ing song,
  over-
    tones plague the list-
ener the un-
    resolved freq-
  encies
elim-
    inat-
      ing the puls-
ing elec-
  trical
cur-
  rent, tape
record-
  ing no
more
  a myth, no
more than mag-
  netism, confused
cowboy
  in Swe-
den, the
  blown up
picture
  of the
horn play-
  er look-
ing at
  a woman dressed as a cat,

I came home to find the lights all burn-
ing bright and I was feeling good inside
a friend had seen me through the night
and you know that things that hits you
when you realize you've thrown it far
too high and as I called your name
around the place

Hello
  teenage
Amer-
  ica,
in o-
  ther words
we of-
  ten read
argu-
  ments of
author-
  ity
in our
  circles,
on our
  ciga-
rette sized
  transis-
tor rad-
  ios,
the mask, *walking*
  home, 5 am, signals
turned, without cars

august moon, 5 am, walking
home, though it's
    too far, "We would
  construct home-
made strobe lights
    by cut-
ting a
  circle in a round wheel
            that spun on a
          fan motor in front
          of a floodlight.
      We would mount black lights
        around the stage
      and draw designs on our
          army surplus jackets and pants
        with florescent paint so we would glow.
      We would harvest huge
sunflowers that grew
          in the wild behind
        the church and place them strategically
    among the equipment and drums, here there was
      a gold-
en throne
  with a
tree-trunk
  of skin
and flesh,
  with an
eye on
  the top, he
saw his grand-

father des-
cending the
    stairs, he came
upon a bur-
    ial mound
and began
    to dig, he
saw a large ra-
    diolarian,
he settled
    for science,
that ques-
    tion from
the 30s, what
    is the
power
    of the
individual
    against
the voice
    of a
whole
    people?

These Necrotic

Ethos Come

the Plains

Bugonia

"... and this is Mezentius, as fashioned by my hands"

The field schemes and friends
and I reduce in terror, become distant
prosceniums. I see Farhad is happy in
two places at once—Boston and Oakland.
I'll never move to those places again.
No one sings peace except in harmony;
counterpoint hardens perception
and makes projection intimate. For instance,
"I spend my days convincing my friends
of my unhappiness and love of commercial
music from the 1960s, when the radio
learned color from the young people, finally."
We bounded time.
Again, mud-black things speak,
covered in something like smoke or living
pelts. We bounded time. The slight echo
of a border foregrounds its love-sound:
part green, part lotion, part biography.
I am not a person, I am a shield,
structured and decorated by
a god of fire. I am inlaid,
I am movement, I am impenetrable folk,
small towns of people who speak with
no irony and argue over things and
how they are made and these objects

act and my body arbitrates to allow
them bounded space in the deep wood
and I am of that deep wood,
I am a shield,
structured and decorated by a god of fire.
I am an object made and we are bound together.
I am so flush with
skin that I offer it to speak.
Location! Hysterical living! I am a shield!

§

Let loose playfulness,
skin to quarrel with systems and paths
that are not and never will be.
I am sheep, cow, horse focused,
insistent, damp and winsome and I guess
magazines wood calculates: gardens, food, living, interiors,
preservation, republic, parabola.
We who too often confuse horror with sympathy,
now we play to feed palms, viral reeds,
horn corsets; all points are large
when marble breathes.
I will lead a procession
to this library of Providence.
What wasn't bees was myth
describing how to grow bees
out of rotting hide.
I am a terrible liar.
I am concrete.
Who hears this book, this object leveled

like a plate? Isn't it stunning, frequent, white?
Characters are residual—the dim light, the
cool wood that means motion backwards into
the vortex: to be, as a to
be, as an us. One's
innards areas the hint of
recorded sound.
I am a library impossibly navigated.
I am brief, mild, and lacking serif.
My entryway is a hacking, nominal thing.
I offer a view between courage and homeopathy—
a sinister touch that grimes the throat.
There is a piano here,
and a place to listen
to music. Stairs and geometries.
There is no newspaper in
this room, only tomorrow squinting.
How strong is this brick?
The Sybill leads us through
openings to the shadows.
I want walls, I want matter.
Her arms light static instead
and our movement is fast
through the dark. The young
man in the next room
hears everything played back in his voice.
Diffusion is suburban, a moustache
drawn on a burrito. What thoughts I had,
my eyes closed, being led
into hell. Pictures rotate and, embodied
in beating, we see what objects see.

Two are brought together and
forefront histories are brought together.
Approach noise as a green people
strung into collections of sitting.
War drawn, war spoken.
Who will receive intimacy
from this book?

§

I remember my fingers tasting like fog.
Someone is playing music,
there is smoke and people moving.
We pass him again thinking,
"What if I double my
voice and harmonize with myself?
How long after I begin
singing will I look out
to see columns built by
men dressed as lizards who
lick earth to make mud-dirt
into clay into bricks? What
happens when information is no
longer sensual, my arms wrapped
around you and what it
means to enfold?

§

Our tattoos label us as citizens.

Leading is a form a remembrance

that turns your body into

ironic distance. One is not

Caesar, one loves Caesar, one

will never be Caesar, one

must birth the new Caesar,

one hates Caesar and I type,

"I was educated in Milan and then Rome.

The thorny lioness loops sequins around the wolf,

his loops seek the children of Pan,

the flowering cytisus is sought by this lascivious child,

and Corydon, you Alexis."

I remember my fingers tasting like fog.

What isn't right is leaving

town for a better town.

What if we just described the town?

Among us this statue distorts.

Fire escapes her eyes and she sweats

and glitches of her lived in form flicker

three times loosely waving a sword.

Odd Sympathy

A curtain of snake prints hangs from the ark-bottomed ceiling,

ancestral statements settle inwards and around

your eyes on the woman's dress,

your hand tucked in your shirt

fingers a bridge, leveled, sweating, anguish

of maturity everyone ignores and erases.

Erase anguish in space, room dimension,

supratemporal bricks the composer has written in the program:

"As there are 'objects,' they are

not a second principle of being

but compositions themselves;

the all is invaded by the score.

An honest microphone. Sugared and tense.

Not erasing or limiting, indeed continuing,

but decreasing in time, rather than space.

The voice separate from the body as a projective force.

Recording translates the body into voice [so,]

what would it mean to mic an object?

One not played by a person,

engaged with and different from a

field recording, where the

microphone takes on the persona of

a dull, listening body?

Points of view add up, moments from the field

happen in a moment.

Listening intent displaces

swans breathing with heads
allied with my own. The courageous
act of water. A past without crackle,
rendered in the first person
in a tense that is very nearly present."

A deep focused set:
  a cave overlooks ocean,
a cloud floats (wires connect it
  to the ceiling), A
large rock.

When you touch something in the dark,
it is the same as seeing it in the light.
Sight and touch are moved by the same cause,
and I listen too, but do not touch objects
you touch. Sound informs at a distance
and our touch limits this pure diamond
of dead star. When you hear
something in the dark it is
the same as seeing it in the light,
the kinaesthetic center of the thing,
those keys we hit that sing
phases of being elsewhere.
I'm always struck by the enormous
sort of magic one feels when looking at
the tradition of an effects knob
that changed the sound of music.
Or, maximum life span in amount of violence
done to original source.
Last night you saw her again—

in a car on the passenger side.
"I kissed your face and then I
said goodbye," said Kathryn.
"I never realized you were crying,"
she said, "Love is worth all
of the sad things it brings, please,
take me back I love you, I
heard you haven't got the time /
time." "I've a house in Scotland,"
Geoffrey said from the driver's seat.
Where do you get this from?
I get it from the things themselves.
I am living death.
Distance becomes growth
from subterranean vibrations
of passionate music,
the inward note sung,
"Standing out in the night,"
the inward note transposed and sung,
"The god of vegetation myths is dead."
Our little sins, our little conclusions
from capillary actions, our little vine
that grows out of the stage while
the conductor walks to his place.

The music begins, two doves fly,
land in the cloud, sing:

"The moon, by
 a radius
drawn to

the center
of the
  earth, directed
to the
  earth, describes
areas proportional
  to the
times.

        &

"It is an
  inherent force
of matter,
  it is
the power
  of resisting
which every
  body perseveres."

        &

"It is
  unmoving planes,
proportional to
  the times
in which
  the motion
of the
  pendulum is
in a circle."

&

"I have
  tested this
with gold,
  silver, lead,
glass, sand,
  common salt,
wood, water,
  and wheat."

&

"I got
  two wooden
boxes, round
  and equal.
I filled
  one of
them with
  wood, I
suspended the
  same weight
for gold
  in the
center of
  oscillation of
the other."

&

"Then, when
  placed close
to each
  other and
set into
  vibration, they
kept swinging
  back and
forth together
  with equal
oscillations for
  a very
long time—
  so it was
for the
  rest of
the materials."

&

"Dependance by definition;
  firmament held for
so long by ether lit
  from above by
ochre root."

&

"The sun comes
  out again and
a squid disappears
  into a tree."

The cloud sings:

"Only don't
  you look
for bodies
  in figures,
where all members
  shine equally
with nothing
  missing."

          &

"There's no
  lack of
vacuum ceasing
  light."

          &

The universe
  could not
suffer so
  much fire
if all its
  starry members
filled all
  with fire."

          &

"Those nature
  subtracted from
the fire, nature spared,
content to distinguish its forms
  by simply showing constellations
with certain stars."

        &

"Outlines designate
  form and fire
answers fire."

        &

"The middle is believed
  from the end
and the end is known highest:
  Nature is satisfied
if all is not hidden."

All sing:

"One such will be who,
  lost in the gulf,
you will seek;
  one head will be lost
for many heads."

The cloud turns black,
the birds fly separately off,

and in the distance is a ship
and on the deck Palinurus looks upwards,
to see what makeup the heavens bring,
what surfaces need to be interpreted today,
what light hides,
what cosmology might be.
Heavy rain halos the sky:
night, monsoon, and dark waves.
Palinurus sings from the high stern:

"Oh! Why has such thick rain
  encircled the sky? What,
Father Neptune, are you doing?"

Turning upstage, he quietly begs the men to lean into the oars,
then turns and sings again:

"Great Aeneas, not even if Jupiter
  promises help
could we hope to get to Italy
  with this sky. It has changed,
it has risen to turn us
  around, it screams from its
black stars.
  Struggling is no use.
  Fortune transcends us,
we should follow its screams to turn.
Your brother Eryx and the Sicilian ports are close,
  if memory of older measurements
line up with the stars
  I measure again."

From deep in the ship, upstage, Aeneas sings:

"Pendulums rot the moon-den
  of the dignified fox
who hates all love.
  What hunch becomes a
lean when we watch
  each other determined to
be casual? Our bodies
  unsymmetrical, limping
here goes age,
  cared father care."

&

"I am carrying my father and the household gods."

&

"I am leading my son out of the city, he is frightened."

&

"I have seen his mother, my wife, talking as a dead woman."

&

"Three times I try to bring her close."

The majesty of the blues, replete
with feral shrieks. The cloud lightens,

and the music steered by the fraught
inward captain now steers itself,
tones emboldening thought emboldening tones,
I just wanna sit here and watch you undress.
We were toying with playing the same
song over and over again throughout
the day. *Urban Bee-Keeping*,
over and over, Kathryn, on the
phone in the living room says,
"Of course," she says, "Of course,
there's no reason to wait
until the results are tangible."
"Of course," she says, "Opera in a garden."
The strangeness of Geoffrey's
blooming gestures, his tan, his dark
tan. A suburban approximation mystifying what happened—
Geoffrey's tye-died muscle shirt wet from the glistening dew—
a serious person defending a serious position,
after the explanation of the term
and before the explicative commentary.
A retrieval of orality.
It wasn't encouraging, Kathryn's use
of the word "horticulture,"
on the phone, in the living room.
Now we are back here. Resorting to
concrete imagery; the boat slowly comes
downstage, towards the rock
but not touching it. The ship
is still, Palinurus stands
and we see him in
full for the first time.

Geoffrey's drums and Aaron's saxophone
are recorded on magnetic tape.
Kathryn, on the phone in the living room,
"I raise my hand when I want the bus to
stop," Kathryn on the phone
in the living room.
The sun's trumpet, the spiral
honey, our ears asking for bigger
acoustical sensations—-zooming closer
through your rushing waves.
All your rushing waves.
With the Moon almost at its mid-point,
limbs relax and the sailors stretch out
with their oars on the hard benches.
Sleep comes down from the sky,
and splits the air into shadows.
You, Palinurus, are preoccupied
with this sad passage; on the high stern
sits god-like Phorbus who sings:

"Palinurus, the fleet bears
  itself at even level.
The air bears
  itself at even level.
It is time to rest."

    &

"Put your head down.
  Close your eyes."
I will take your post."

Barely raising his eyes, Palinurus sings:

"Do you tell me
  to be quiet
in ignorance of the calm
  and resting face
of the sea?"

        &

"You think I have
  confidence in this
monster here?"

        &

"Aeneas doesn't
  deserve to be
deceived by a phony wind
  and a cheating sky."

But anger becomes accident,
Palinurus slumps down on the damp wood
and Sleep chucks him face first
(flying with wires) into the water
and so the world begins. The atoms fill up
space slowly and, without guarantee,
choose partners based on dignity
and beauty, collective beauty,
love comes from space and not

time and so things find other things unworried,
like and unlike, equal and unequal,
large and larger they become throughout
space with every moment without
name without number. What it
is like before Melody!
To know only note and then
only counterpoint between phantasms,
layers of un-decaying hues that build
fear until Moment, gasseous
and sexed, lemmatizes redolence. It follows,
coming to sail, rising behind the deck.
In rivalry, its partners strike the sea
and sweep the surface.
Sleep has highjacked my ship.
His face is blue, he is carrying balloons,
her hands stretched deep into the sea,
attached to my head.
The curtain falls on the sea.
Next act, the rock.

§

The rock waits upon the stage.
What makes sense procures.
Rock draws, it leads. Music begins.
A woman appears upstage and points:

"When the new
  god comes,
we surrender dumbly,"

&

"Oh, and occasionally,
   the wares are
doubled."

A large urban silverfish bumbles onstage,
sits besides the rock, adjusts itself,
faints against the rock
awakes slightly to the swell,
faints again, and sings:

"A vessel full
   of ashes can
take as much water
   as it does
when empty."

"I kissed your face
and then said goodbye," says Kathryn,
lying in the bath. "I never realized
you were crying," she says, "Love is
worth all of the sad things it brings,
please, take me back I love you,
I heard you haven't got the
time / time." What horrible motion
the voice gives to the standard,
what horrible motion the violinist
gives to the bow, while under the
ingenious lustre of this singular temple,
awaiting the queen, here beneath,

what urbane fortune and artifice has been interpreted
by hands that labored, worked, and mirrored
he sees, growing wildly, carved from rock,
a temple handsomely polished,
rising from the stage floor underneath
the silverfish who sings,
held by the rising temple:

"Object detection,
   localization,
using texture
is a different
   way of making,
a different way
   of hearing
than beginning
   in a forest."

        &

"A precipitous detail,
   a focusing noun
is all music needs.
The color, the speed,
   the texture, the
forest calls us,
lays bear
   its synthesis,
its detail."

        &

"The corridors
  the mind
stretches through
  this to make
a hovel
  how far inwards
to head except
  to say inwards."

            &

"Inwards, more,
  thoughtfulness,
more alone, more
  furious silence,
You! who make
  me incapable
of expression,
  That limit
that furthers
us together, how
  I bleed
into you
  and
stretch sensation."

            &

"I listen, I
  listen, I fulfill
so much,

I could not
contain it
  anymore. I could
not watch out
  for myself."

        &

"I could not
  limit the
expression that
  you have
asked me
  to limit."

        &

"What lousy
  purchase
my brain
  has on
my body!
  What body
is this?
  Latency,
how far
  you have come
in the spaces
  between our bodies."

He falls on the temple's point,

the point engages him, penetrates the costume,

and as the body slides down

the silver temple the chiseled lines

glisten with blood,

and the stage lights brighten the carved stories.

The men, standing there looking at the temple,

read themselves,

see Iliam's pugil order—-

known, famous, total, vulgar, terror,

Atreus' sons, Priam, Achilles.

Constituted, lachrymose,

Aeneas sings:

"Is there any place,

  Achates, any kingdom

on this dark earth

  not filled with

our sad labors?

  And Priam!

Here, too, labor

  also finds praise;

here too, tearful,

  mortal things

touch the mind.

  Solve your fear;

fame will bring

  salvation to you."

So he sings, and feeds his mind

on the empty pictures, with multiple

sighs and a river on his face eroding
tendencies in the rock. Kathryn says,
"So now you have to choose
between my two (black) lungs / never forget
you have a choice / hide yourself
in the woods / at that time
I guess we misunderstood / inthegraves."
The window became so wet
I couldn't see so I ran
downstairs as I was and slipped out
the back into the poor garden and
there was Geoffrey there was poor
Geoffrey at the end of the garden shivering,
this name, this sign, indexed to
the void, a pure, proper, musical,
name. Later, when all have gone,
and in turn the moon oppresses her light
and the setting stars suggest sleep
alone in the empty house she grieves and
falls on the couch he left.
He is absent, she is absent from him,
she hears him, she sees him
holds Ascanius on her lap, imagining,
captivated by his father, detaining
a passion deceiving and unspeakable.
No longer rise the begun towers,
no longer do the youth exercise their arms
or prepare the ports and bulwarks for safety in war;
the work is pending and interrupted—
threatening great walls and machines
that touch the sky. Later, the guests gone,

the moon dark, and the stars set
she grieves alone in the empty house
and falls on his abandoned couch.
He is absent, she is absent from him,
she hears him, she sees him,
holds Ascanius on her lap, imagining,
captivated by his father, detaining a passion
deceiving and unspeakable. After all leave,
and the moon obscures her light
and the setting stars suggest sleep
a woman slowly walks onstage, sings:

"Underneath the earth
  is a building
filled with the seeds
  of all things."

    &

"Little leaves, extensions
  of living rot, limits
of sequence."

Wood, old wood. Kathryn, the telephone
keeps ringing. These people so full of holes,
their heads so full of holes.
Geoffrey woke up. The thickness
of this man's hands. "Any questions,

useless," he said with his fingers
to his lips. It wasn't the time.
And Geoffrey started to cry.
Wearing
a pair of old jeans and an
army-type anorak, I had
a hamburger and a cup of
tea in a cafe. "I
wanna show you the
different emotions," she says, lying in
the bath, waiting for you and me.
"Look at them over there
with their 'arches.' You
just can't trust them."
I think of nothing else.
What about dreams made out of things?

"Zooming closer
 through cranking
all your
 rushing waves,
the spell works, VISION
 with Geoffrey,
all your
 rushing waves,
the spell works, SOUND
with Kathryn, who
 might be alive, she
is full of story, she shows
 you'll be alright."

NOTES

Large sections of both "Bugonia" and "Odd Sympathy" were composed during a residency at *AS220*, Providence. This residency also provided me with the opportunity to print a small edition of *The Resonant Space* on an offset printer. Thanks to Neal. An early form of "Bugonia" appeared online as part of the Dallas Biennial Volume One. Thanks to Michael, Jesse, and Stephen. "Bugonia" and "Odd Sympathy" were both performed at A Slender Gamut, Brooklyn as part of *Rehearsal for Grand Opera for One Person*, a collaboration with Caroline Picard. Thanks to Matthew.

Much of this text is sifted from and in response to reading material from over a five year period. These texts need not be apparent to the reader, but I must acknowledge two ancient writers—Lucretius and Virgil—and one modern—Graham Harman—for inspiring the main argument of "Odd Sympathy." A performance of Strauss and Hofmannsthal's *Ariadne auf Naxos* at the Lyric Opera of Chicago during their 2011–2012 season was also key in inspiring the staging of sections from *The Aeneid* that appear here.

Kenning Editions

Kenningeditions.com